CHART HITS OF 2014-2015
FOR UKULELE

ISBN 978-1-4950-1237-2

HAL•LEONARD®
CORPORATION
7777 W. BLUEMOUND RD. P.O. BOX 13819 MILWAUKEE, WI 53213

Visit Hal Leonard Online at
www.halleonard.com

All About That Bass

Words and Music by Kevin Kadish and Meghan Trainor

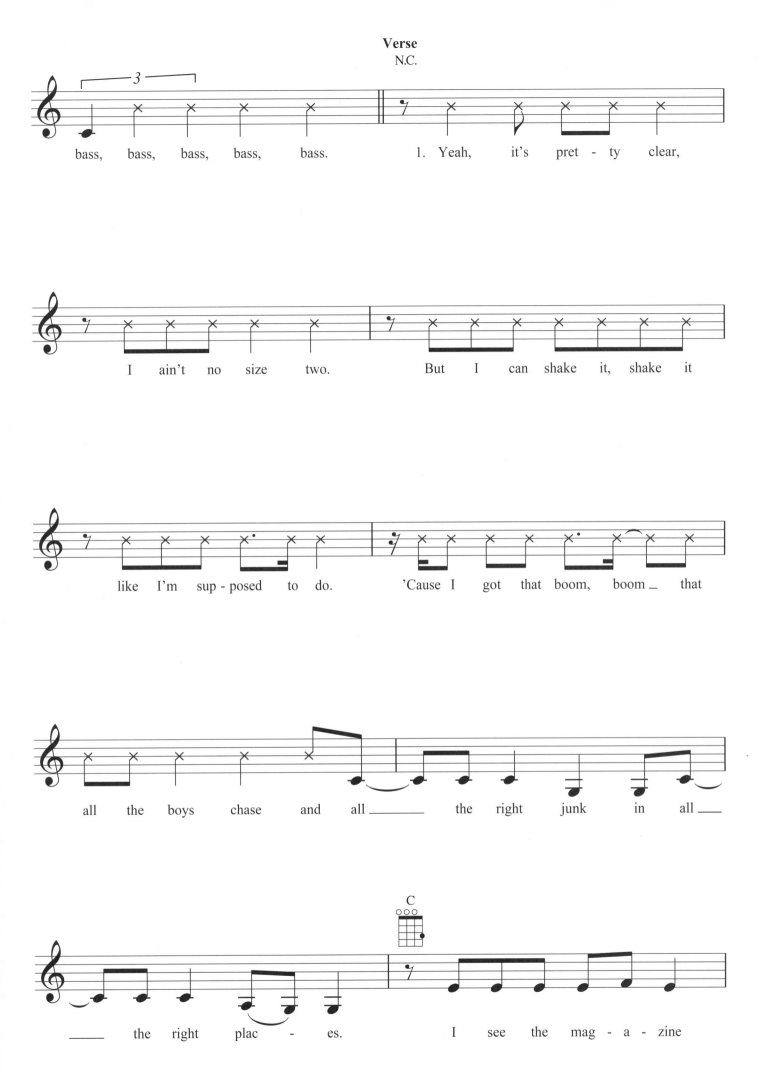

Verse

N.C.

bass, bass, bass, bass, bass.

1. Yeah, it's pret-ty clear,

I ain't no size two.

But I can shake it, shake it

like I'm sup-posed to do.

'Cause I got that boom, boom _ that

all the boys chase and all _____ the right junk in all ___

C

_____ the right plac - es.

I see the mag - a - zine

3

work - in' that Pho - to - shop. _ We know that sh** ain't _ real. _

_ C' - mon now, make it stop. If you got beau - ty, beau - ty,

just raise 'em up 'cause ev - 'ry inch of you is per - fect from the

Pre-Chorus

bot - tom to the top. Yeah, my ma - ma, _ she told me, _ "Don't

wor - ry _ a - bout your size." _

She says, "Boys like _ a lit - tle _ more

boo - ty ____ to hold at night." ____

You know I won't be ____ no stick fig - ure,

sil - i - cone Bar - bie doll. ____ So, if

that's what ___ you're in - to, ____ then go a - head ___ and move a - long. ___

Be - cause you know I'm

Chorus

all a - bout that bass, 'bout that bass. No tre - ble. I'm

all a - bout that bass, 'bout that bass. No treb - le. I'm

all a - bout that bass, 'bout that bass. No treb - le. I'm

To Coda ⊕

all a - bout that bass, 'bout that bass, hey. 2. I'm bring - in'

Verse

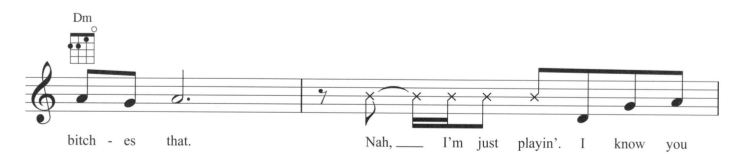

boo - ty back. _____ Go a - head and tell them skin - ny

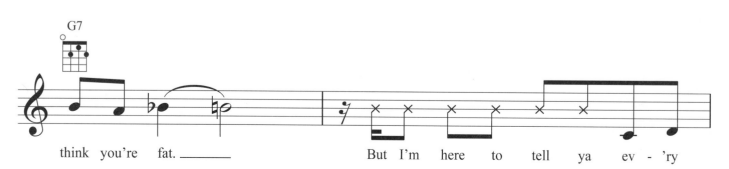

bitch - es that. Nah, _____ I'm just playin'. I know you

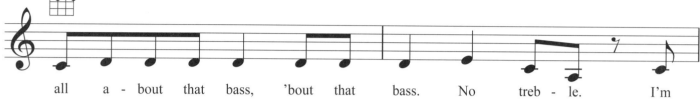

think you're fat. _____ But I'm here to tell ya ev - 'ry

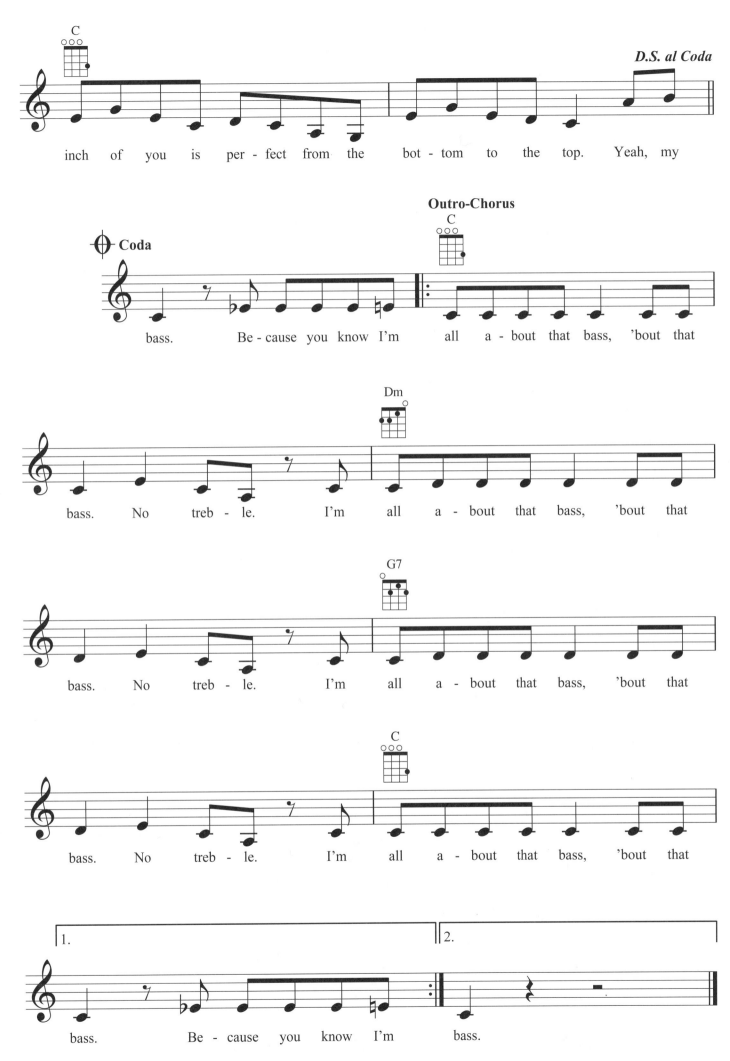

inch of you is per - fect from the bot - tom to the top. Yeah, my

Outro-Chorus

Coda

bass. Be - cause you know I'm all a - bout that bass, 'bout that

bass. No treb - le. I'm all a - bout that bass, 'bout that

bass. No treb - le. I'm all a - bout that bass, 'bout that

bass. No treb - le. I'm all a - bout that bass, 'bout that

1.

2.

bass. Be - cause you know I'm bass.

Animals

Words and Music by Adam Levine, Ben Levin and Shellback

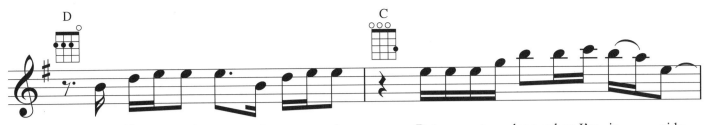

It's like we can't stop; we're en - e - mies. But we get a - long when I'm in - side __
You're still in my head, for - ev - er stuck. So you can do what you wan - na do. __

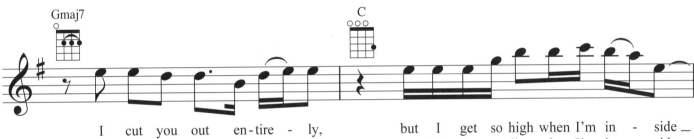

___ you. ___ (Hey.) You're like a drug that's kill - ing me.
(Hey.) I love your lies; I'll eat 'em up,

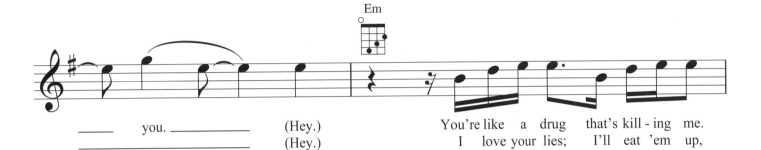

I cut you out en - tire - ly, but I get so high when I'm in - side __
but don't de - ny the an - i - mal that comes a - live when I'm in - side __

Pre-Chorus

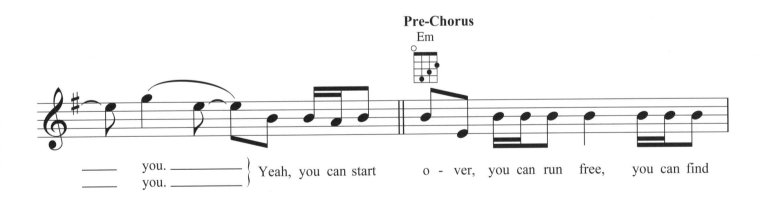

___ you. ___ } Yeah, you can start o - ver, you can run free, you can find
___ you. ___

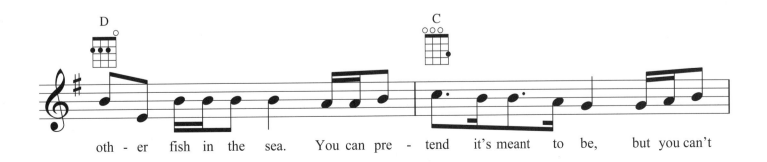

oth - er fish in the sea. You can pre - tend it's meant to be, but you can't

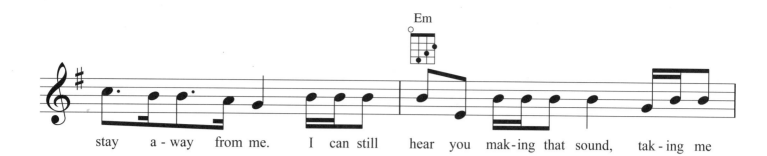

stay a - way from me. I can still hear you mak-ing that sound, tak-ing me

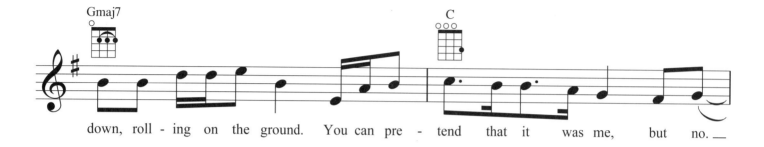

down, roll - ing on the ground. You can pre - tend that it was me, but no. __

𝄋 **Chorus**

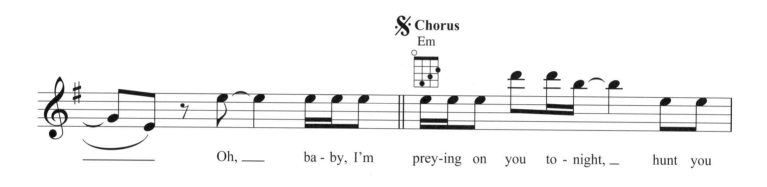

__ Oh, __ ba - by, I'm prey-ing on you to - night, __ hunt you

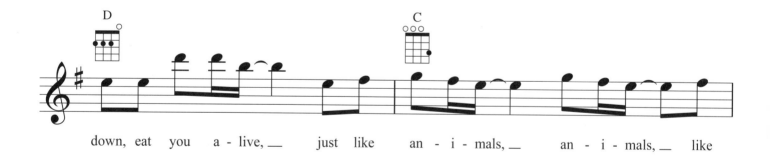

down, eat you a - live, __ just like an - i - mals, __ an - i - mals, __ like

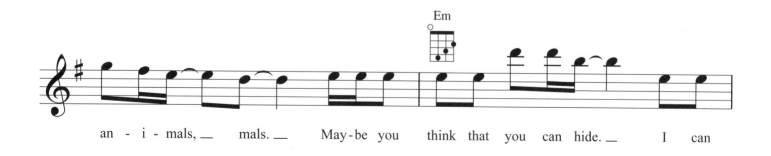

an - i - mals, __ mals. __ May-be you think that you can hide. __ I can

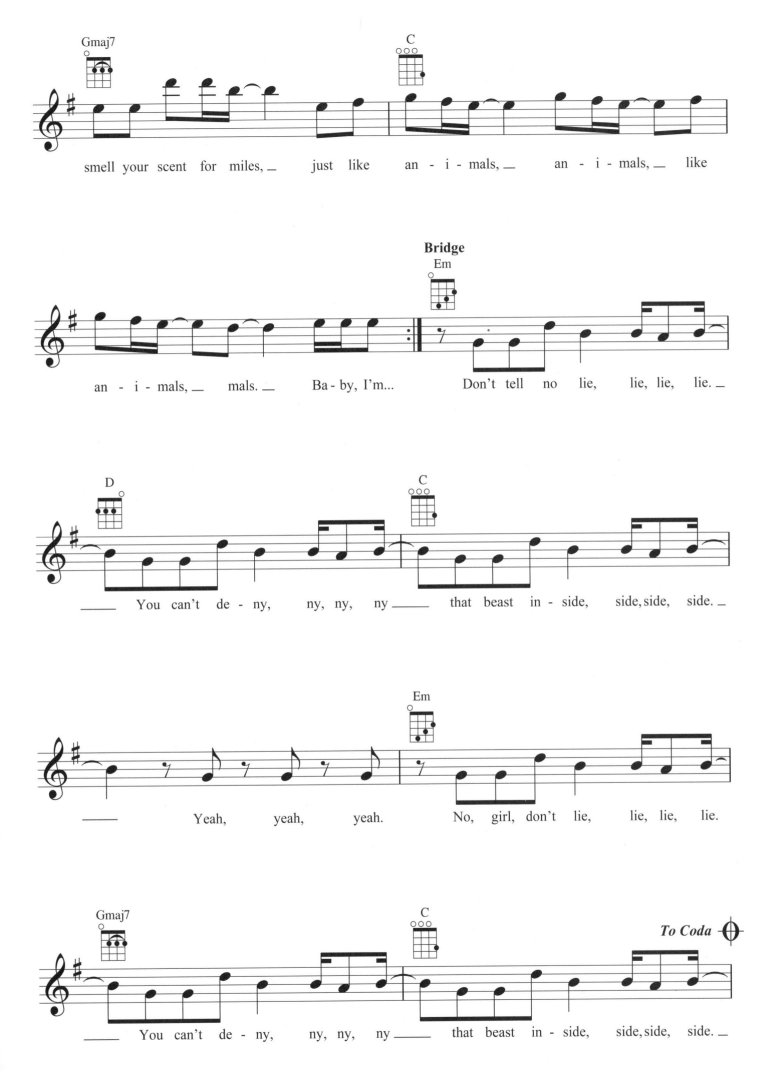

All of Me

Words and Music by John Stephens and Toby Gad

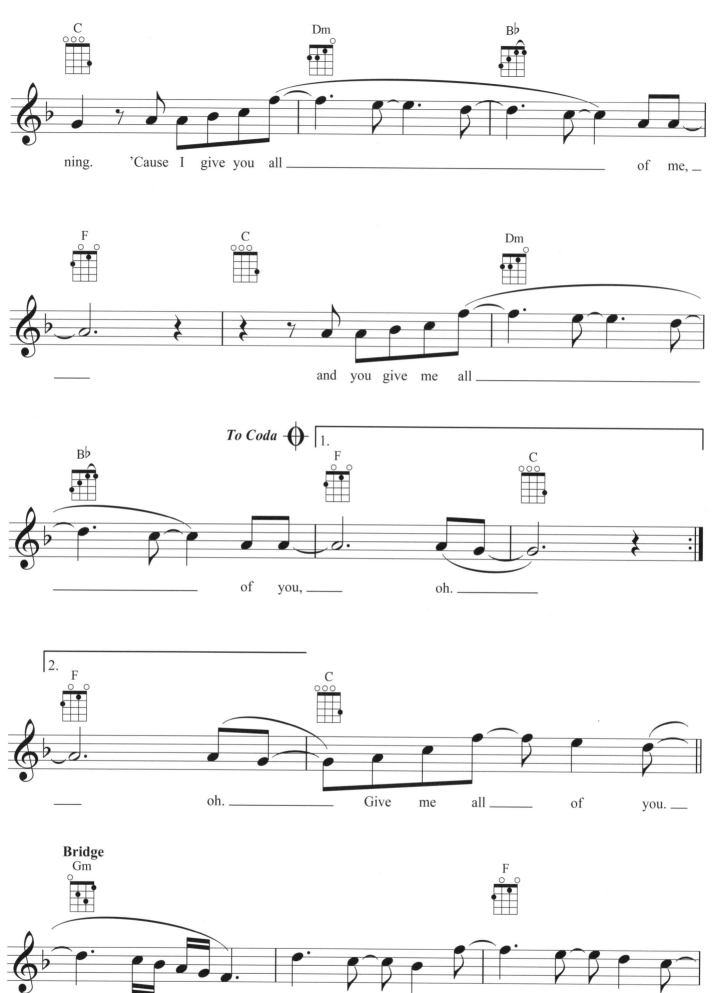

Don't

Words and Music by Ed Sheeran, Dawn Robinson, Ben Levin,
Raphael Saadiq, Ali Jones-Muhammad and Conesha Owens

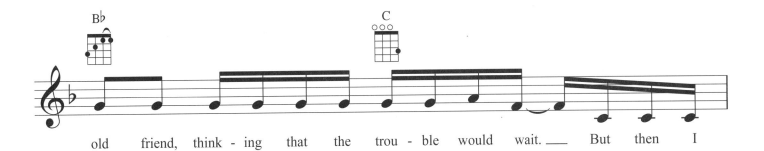

old friend, think - ing that the trou - ble would wait. ___ But then I

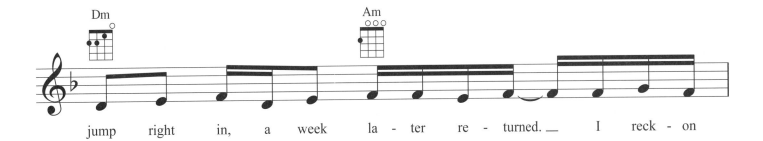

jump right in, a week la - ter re - turned. ___ I reck - on

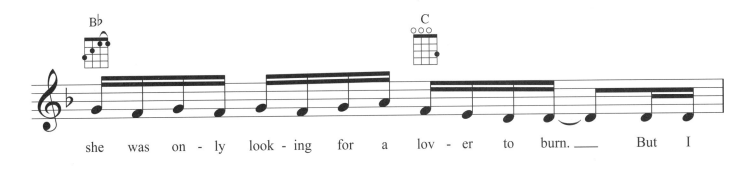

she was on - ly look - ing for a lov - er to burn. ___ But I

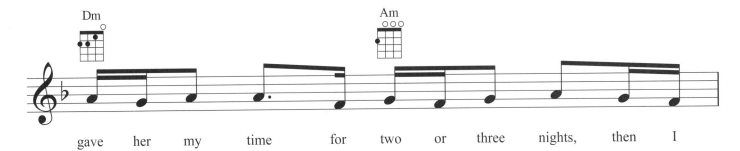

gave her my time for two or three nights, then I

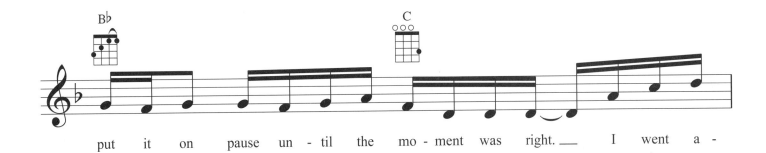

put it on pause un - til the mo - ment was right. ___ I went a -

way for months un - til our paths ___ crossed a - gain. ___ She told me,

"I was nev-er look-ing for a friend. May-be you can

swing by my room a-round ten. Ba - by, bring the

lem - on and a bot - tle of gin. We'll be in be - tween the

sheets till the late a. m." Ba - by, if you want - ed

me, then you should -'ve just said. She's sing-ing: Ah, la 'n la _____ la.
Don't **** with my

Chorus

love. That heart is so cold all o - ver my

home. ___ I don't wan-na know that, ___ babe. Ah, la 'n la _____ la.
Don't **** with my

love. I told her, she knows. Take aim and re -

To Coda ⊕ 1.

load. ___ I don't wan-na know that, ___ babe. Ah, la 'n la _____ la.
2. For a cou-ple

2.
D.S. al Coda

Ah, la 'n la _____ la.

⊕ **Coda**

Ah, la 'n la _____ la.
Don't**** with my

Outro-Chorus

love. That heart is so cold all o-ver my

home. ____ I don't wan-na know that, ___ babe.   Ah,   la   'n   la _____ la.
Don't **** with my

love.   I told her,   she   knows.   Take aim and re -

load. ____ I don't wan-na know that, ___ babe.   Ah,   la   'n   la _____ la.

Additional Lyrics

2. For a couple weeks I only wanna see her.
   We drink away the days with a take-away pizza.
   Before, a text message was the only way to reach her.
   Now she's staying at my place and loves the way I treat her.
   Singing out Aretha all over the track like a feature,
   And never wants to sleep; I guess that I don't want to, either.
   But me and her, we make money the same way:
   Four cities, two planes the same day.
   And those shows have never been what it's about,
   But maybe we'll go together and just figure it out.
   I'd rather put on a film with you and sit on the couch,
   But we should get on a plane or we'll be missing it now.
   Wish I'd have written it down, the way things played out
   When she was kissing him, how I was confused about.
   Now she should figure it out while I'm sat here singing:

3. *(Knock knock knock)* on my hotel door.
   I don't even know if she knows what for.
   She was crying on my shoulder; I already told ya:
   Trust and respect is what we do this for.
   I never intended to be next,
   But you didn't need to take him to bed, that's all.
   And I never saw him as a threat,
   Until you disappeared with him to have sex, of course.
   It's not like we were both on tour.
   We were staying on the same **** hotel floor.
   And I wasn't looking for a promise or commitment,
   But it was never just fun and I thought you were different.
   This is not the way you realize what you wanted.
   It's a bit too much, too late, if I'm honest.
   And all this time, God knows, I'm singing:

Let It Go

from Disney's Animated Feature FROZEN
Music and Lyrics by Kristen Anderson-Lopez and Robert Lopez

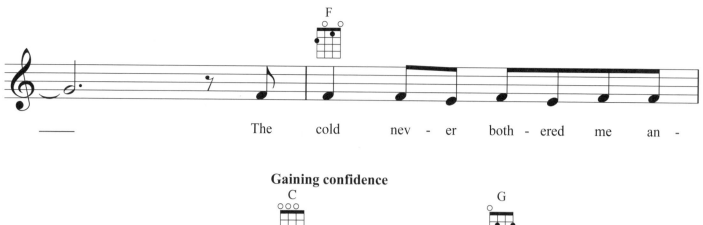

The cold nev - er both - ered me an -

Gaining confidence

y - way.

Verse

2. It's fun - ny how some dis - tance makes

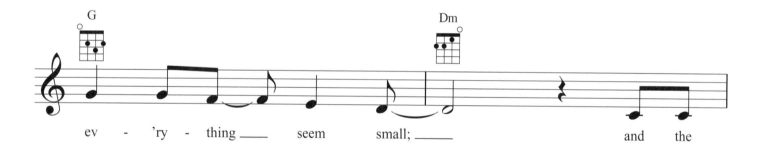

ev - 'ry - thing ___ seem small; ___ and the

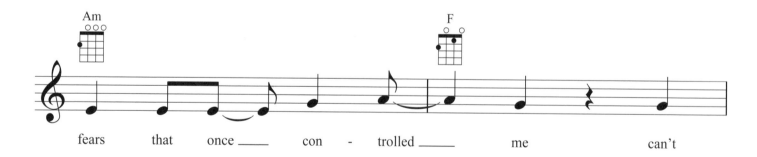

fears that once ___ con - trolled ___ me can't

Pre-Chorus

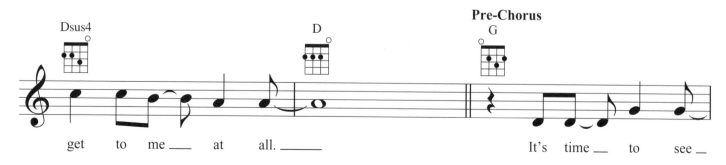

get to me ___ at all. ___ It's time ___ to see ___

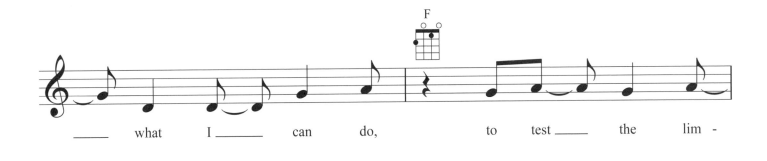

_____ what I _____ can do, to test _____ the lim -

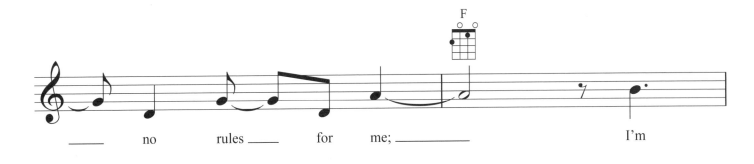

- its and _____ break through. _____ No right, _____ no wrong, _

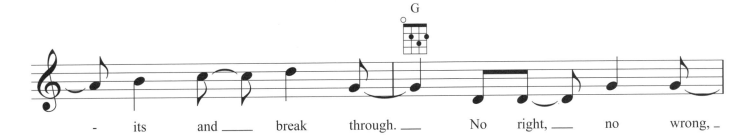

_____ no rules _____ for me; _____ I'm

D.S. al Coda

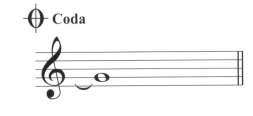

Coda

free! _____ Let it go, _

Bridge

My pow - er flur - ries through _ the air _____

_____ in - to _____ the ground. _ My soul _____ is spi -

-ral - ing _____ in fro - zen frac - tals all _____

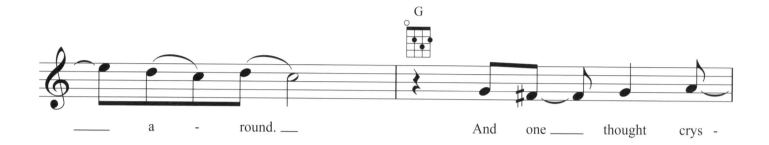

_____ a - round. _____ And one _____ thought crys -

- tal - liz - es like _____ an i - cy blast: _____

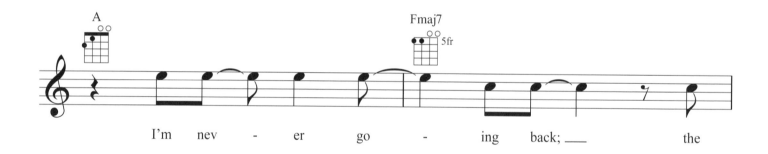

I'm nev - er go - ing back; _____ the

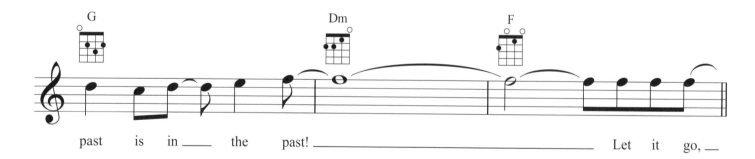

past is in _____ the past! _____ Let it go, _____

Chorus

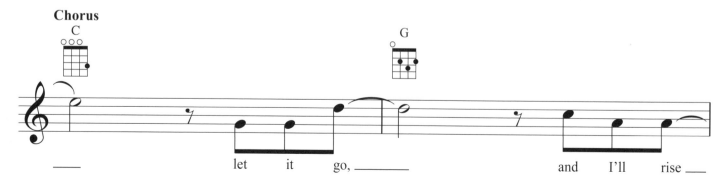

_____ let it go, _____ and I'll rise _____

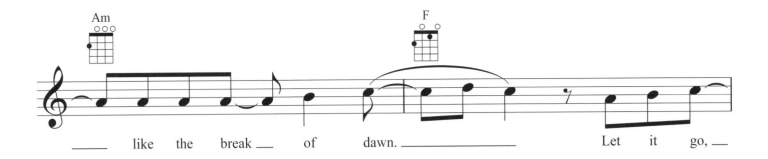

_____ like the break _____ of dawn. _____ Let it go, _____

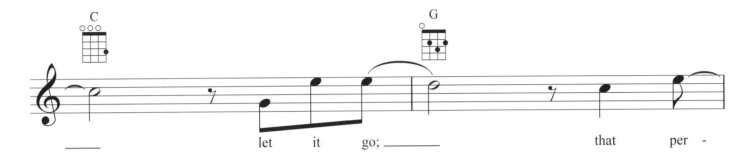

_____ let it go; _____ that per -

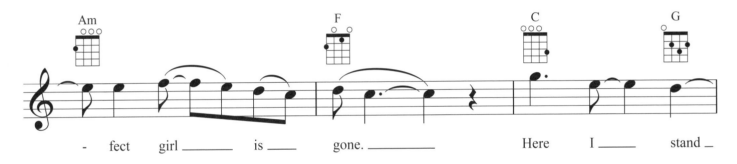

- fect girl _____ is _____ gone. _____ Here I _____ stand _____

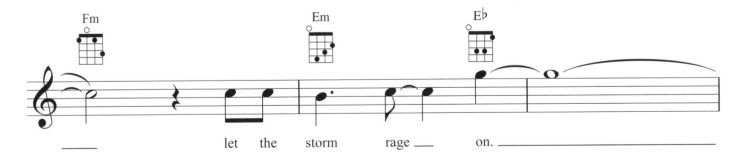

_____ in the light of _____ day; _____

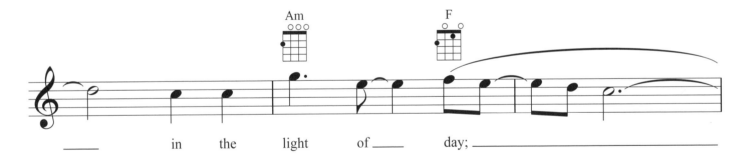

_____ let the storm rage _____ on. _____

_____ The cold nev - er both-ered me an - y - way.

Habits
(Stay High)

Words and Music by Tove Lo, Jakob Jerlström and Ludvig Söderberg

Verse

Bb   Dm

2. I get home, I got the munch - ies, binge on all my
3. Pick up dad - dies at the play - ground, how I spend my

F

Twin - kies; throw up in the tub, then I go to sleep. _
day - time. Loos - en up the frown, make 'em feel a - live. _

Bb   Dm

____ And I drank up all my mon - ey, dazed and kind - a
____ I'll make it fast and greas - y; I'm numb and way too

F   N.C.

lone - ly.⎫
eas - y.⎭   You're gone and __ I got - ta stay

𝄉 Chorus

Bb   Dm

high all the time _____ to keep you off my

F

mind, ooh, _____ ooh. _____

31

High all the time ____ to keep you off my mind, ooh, ____

ooh. ____ Spend my days locked in a haze, tryin' to for-get

you, babe. I fall back down. Got-ta stay high all ____ my life __

To Coda ⊕ | 1.

____ to for-get I'm miss-ing you, ooh, ____ ooh.

| 2. **Bridge**

ooh. ____ Stay-ing in my play pre-tend,

where the fun ain't got no end. ____ Oh. __

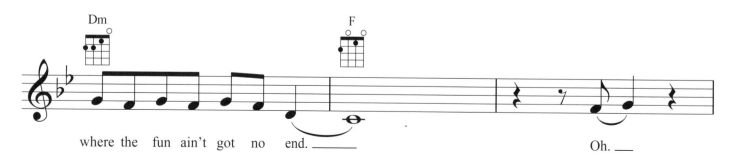

32

Can't go home a - lone a - gain; need some - one to numb the pain. ___

Oh. ___ Stay - ing in my play pre - tend,

where the fun ain't got no end. ___ Ah, oh. ___

Can't go home a - lone a - gain; need some - one to numb the pain. ___

D.S. al Coda

You're gone and ___ I got - ta stay

Coda

ooh. ___ Oh oh.

Happy

from DESPICABLE ME 2
Words and Music by Pharrell Williams

you feel ___ like that's what you wan - na do. ___

𝄋 Bridge

N.C.(A7)

Bring me down, _____ can't noth - in' bring me down; ___

_____ your love is too high. Bring me down, _____ can't noth - in'

1.

bring me down. _____ (Let me tell you now.)

2., 3.   — **Chorus**

Fmaj7

___ I said... (Be - cause I'm hap - py.) Clap a - long if ___

Em7   A7

___ you feel like a room with - out a roof. ___ (Be - cause I'm

Riptide

Words and Music by Vance Joy

First note

Verse
Moderately

Am   G   C

1. I was scared of den - tists and the dark. ____
2. There's this mov - ie that ___ I think you'll like. ____ This

Am   G   C

I was scared of pret - ty girls ___ and start - ing con - ver - sa - tions. _ All ___
guy de - cides to quit his job ___ and heads to New York Cit - y. ___ This

Am   G   C

____ my ___ friends ___ are turn - ing green; ___ you're the
cow - boy's ___ run - ning from him - self, ___ and

Am   G   C

ma - gi - cian's ___ as - sist - ant in their dream. ____ }
she's been liv - ing on ___ the high - est shelf. ____ }

Ah

Pre-Chorus

Am   G   C   Am   G

ooh. ____ Ah oh, ____ and they

Chorus

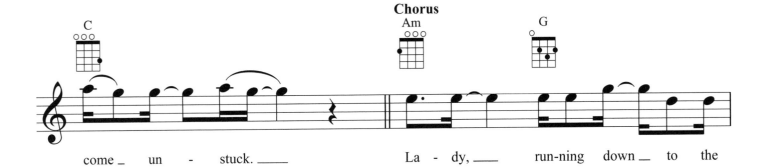

come _ un - stuck. _____ La - dy, ____ run-ning down _ to the

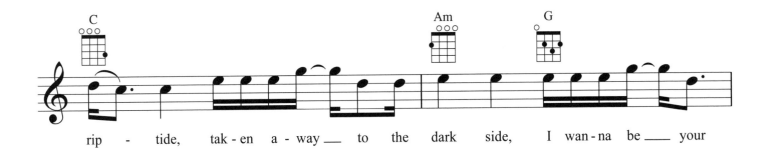

rip - tide, tak - en a - way _ to the dark side, I wan - na be _ your

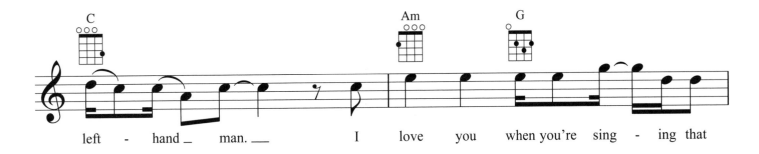

left - hand _ man. _ I love you when you're sing - ing that

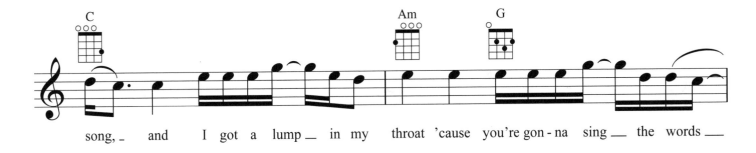

song, _ and I got a lump _ in my throat 'cause you're gon - na sing _ the words _

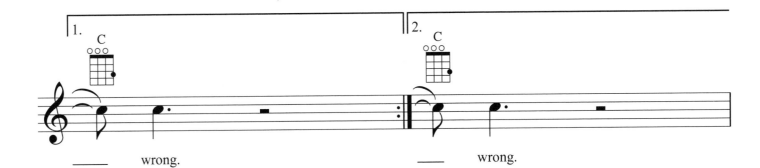

_____ wrong.   _____ wrong.

(Instrumental)

Bridge

I just wan - na, I just wan - na know _____

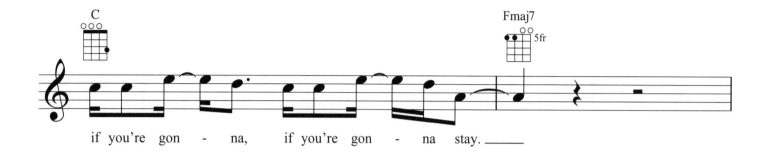

if you're gon - na, if you're gon - na stay. _____

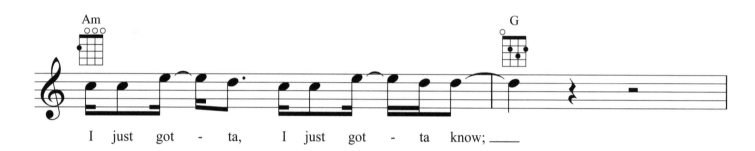

I just got - ta, I just got - ta know; _____

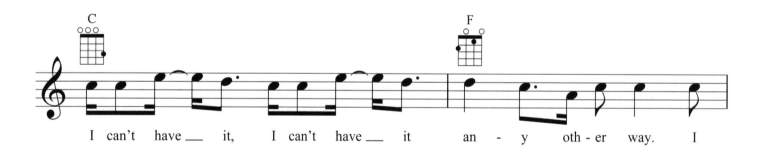

I can't have ___ it, I can't have ___ it an - y oth - er way. I

swear she's des - tined for the screen;

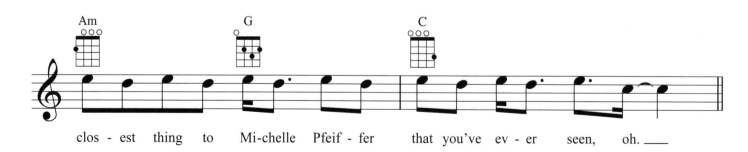

clos - est thing to Mi-chelle Pfeif - fer that you've ev - er seen, oh. ____

Chorus

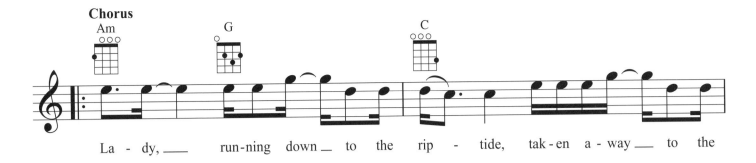

La - dy, ___ run-ning down ___ to the rip - tide, tak - en a - way ___ to the

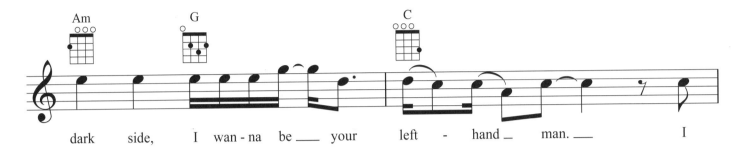

dark side, I wan - na be ___ your left - hand ___ man. ___ I

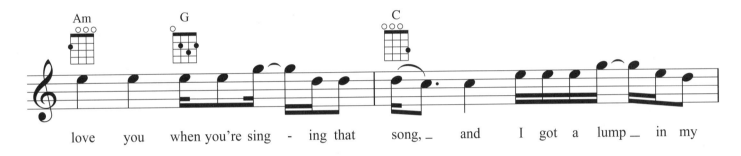

love you when you're sing - ing that song, _ and I got a lump ___ in my

1., 2.

throat 'cause you're gon - na sing ___ the words _____ wrong. Oh,

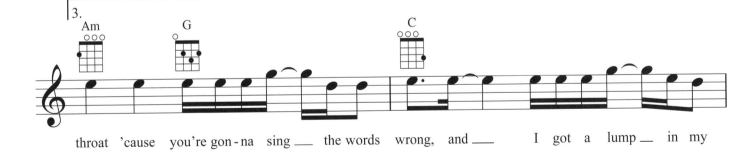

3.

throat 'cause you're gon - na sing ___ the words wrong, and ___ I got a lump ___ in my

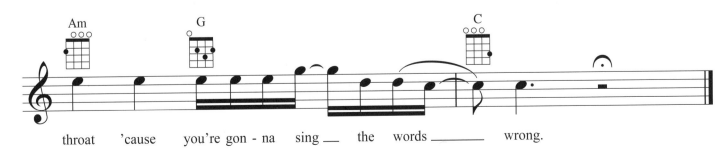

throat 'cause you're gon - na sing ___ the words _____ wrong.

Rude

Words and Music by Nasri Atweh, Mark Pellizzer, Alex Tanas, Ben Spivak and Adam Messinger

'cause I know that you're an old-fash-ioned man.
you know she's in love with me. She will go

Pre-Chorus

an-y-where I go. Can I have your daugh-ter for the rest of my life? __ Say

yes, say yes, 'cause I need to know. You say I'll nev-er get your bless-ing till the

day __ I die. __ Tough luck, my friend, but the an-swer is no. / 'cause the an-swer's still no.

Chorus

Why you got-ta be so rude? _____ Don't you know I'm

hu-man, too? _____ Why you got-ta be so rude? _____

43

I'm gon - na   mar - ry her an - y - way.   Mar - ry that girl,

mar - ry her an - y - way.   Mar - ry that girl, yeah,   no mat - ter what you say.

Mar - ry that girl   and   we'll be a fam - i - ly.   Why you got - ta

To Coda

be   so   rude? _____

Rude. _____

Pre-Chorus

Can   I   have your daugh - ter for the

44

rest of my life? ____ Say yes, say yes, 'cause I

need to know. You say I'll nev - er get your bless - ing till the

D.S. al Coda

day ____ I die. ____ Tough luck, my friend, but no still means no.

Coda

rude? _____ Yeah. ____

Why you got - ta be so rude? _____

Why you got - ta be so rude? ____

Shake It Off

Words and Music by Taylor Swift, Max Martin and Shellback

At least, that's what peo - ple say, _____ mm,
And that's what they don't know, _____ mm,

mm. That's what peo - ple say, _____ mm, mm. But I keep
mm. That's what they don't know, _____ mm, mm. But I keep

Pre-Chorus

cruis - ing; can't stop, won't stop mov - ing. } It's
cruis - ing; can't stop, won't stop groov - ing. }

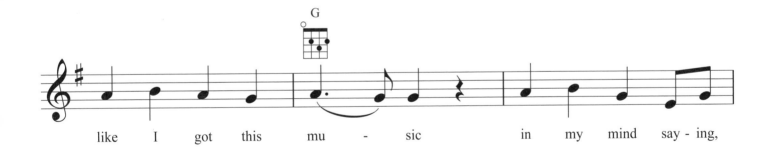

like I got this mu - sic in my mind say - ing,

"It's gon - na be al - right." _____ 'Cause the

off. 2. I nev-er miss a off. (Ooh, _____ ooh!) I shake it off, I shake it

(Ooh, _____ ooh!)

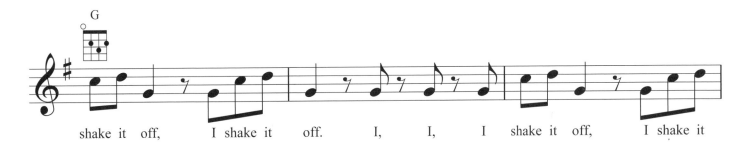

off. I, I, I shake it off, I shake it off. I, I, I

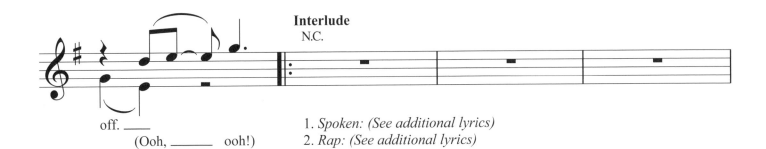

shake it off, I shake it off. I, I, I shake it off, I shake it

off. ____

(Ooh, _____ ooh!)

1. *Spoken: (See additional lyrics)*
2. *Rap: (See additional lyrics)*

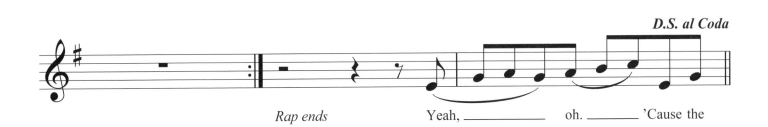

Rap ends   Yeah, _____ oh. _____ 'Cause the

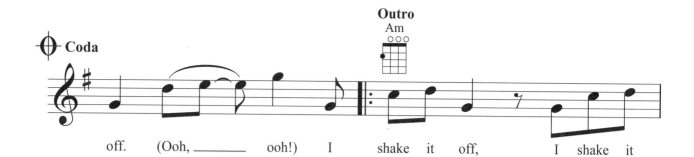

off.   (Ooh, _____ ooh!)   I   shake   it   off,   I   shake   it

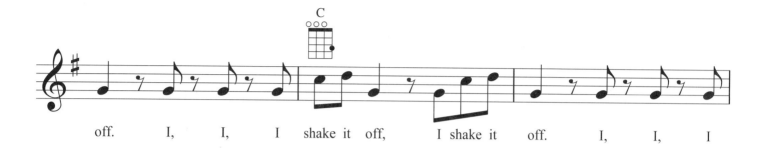

off.   I,   I,   I   shake   it   off,   I   shake   it   off.   I,   I,   I

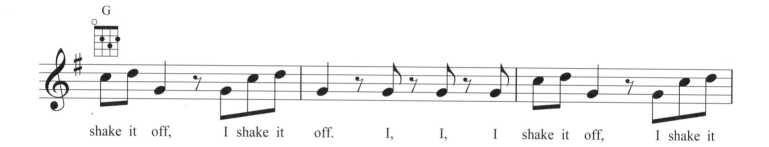

shake   it   off,   I   shake   it   off.   I,   I,   I   shake   it   off,   I   shake   it

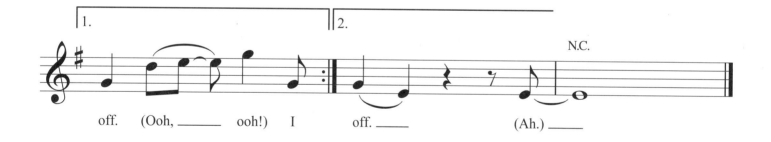

off.   (Ooh, _____ ooh!)   I   off. _____   (Ah.) _____

Additional Lyrics

Spoken: Hey, hey, hey! Just think: While you've been gettin'
Down and out about the liars and the dirty, dirty cheats of the world,
You could've been gettin' down to this sick beat!

Rap: My ex-man brought his new girlfriend.
She's like, "Oh, my god!" But I'm just gonna shake.
And to the fella over there with the hella good hair,
Won't you come on over, baby? We can shake, shake, shake.

Stay with Me

Words and Music by Sam Smith, James Napier and William Edward Phillips

Steal My Girl

Words and Music by Louis Tomlinson, Liam Payne, Julian Bunetta, Wayne Hector, Edward Drewett and John Ryan

1. She be my queen since we ___ were six-teen. We want ___ ___ the same things, we dream ___ the same dreams, al-right.
2. Kiss-es like cream, her walk ___ is so mean, and ev-'ry jaw drop when she's ___ in those jeans, al-right.

Al-right.
Al-right.

I got it all 'cause she ___ is the one. Her mom ___ ___ calls me "love," her dad ___ calls me "son," ___ al-right.
I don't ex-ist if I ___ don't have her. The sun ___ does-n't shine, the world ___ does-n't turn, ___ al-right.

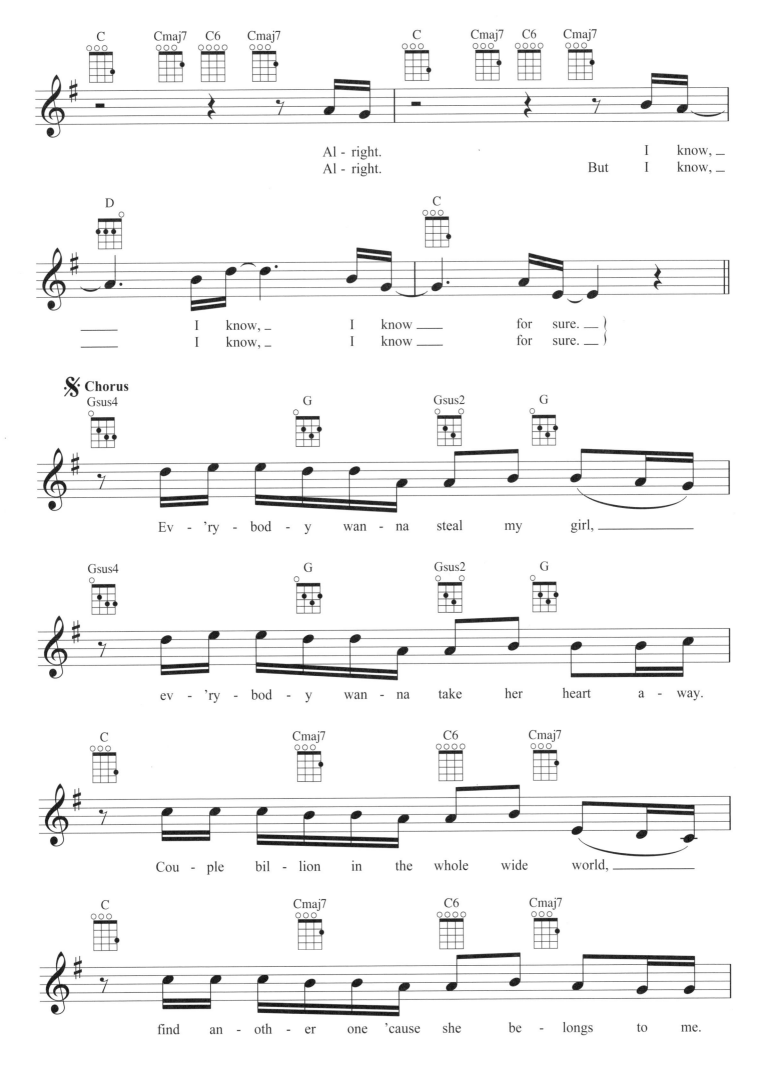

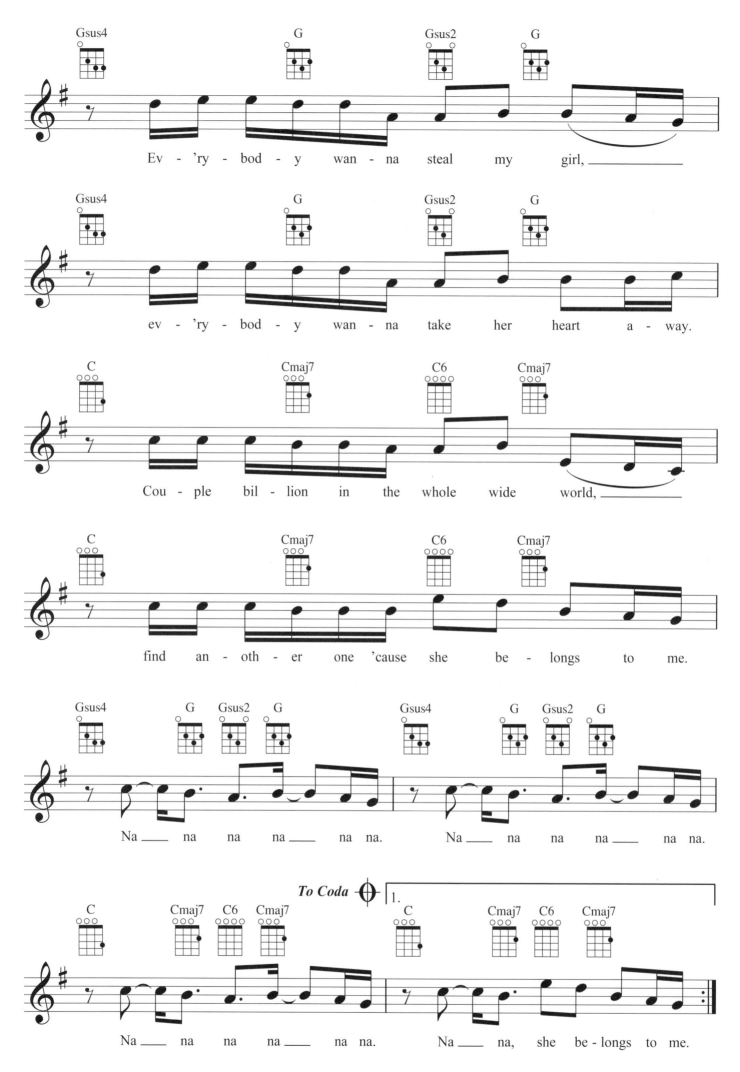

Ev - 'ry - bod - y wan - na steal my girl, _____

ev - 'ry - bod - y wan - na take her heart a - way.

Cou - ple bil - lion in the whole wide world, _____

find an - oth - er one 'cause she be - longs to me.

Na ___ na na na ___ na na. Na ___ na na na ___ na na.

To Coda

1.

Na ___ na na na ___ na na. Na ___ na, she be - longs to me.

56

Na ___ na na na. ___ She knows, ___ she knows ___ that I

nev-er let her down be-fore. ___ She knows, ___ she knows ___ that I'm

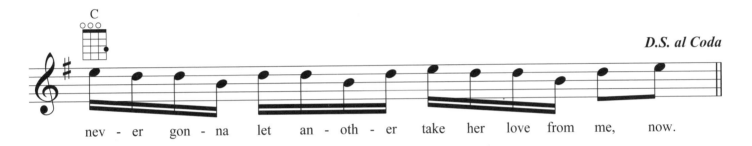

nev-er gon-na let an-oth-er take her love from me, now.

D.S. al Coda

Coda

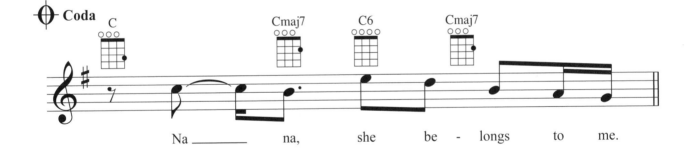

Na ___ na, she be-longs to me.

Outro

Na ___ na na na ___ na na. Na ___ na na na ___ na na.

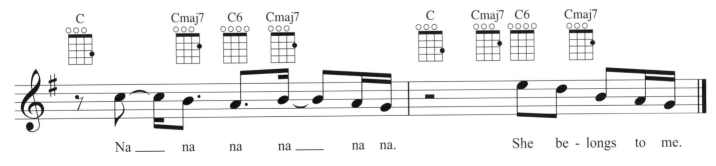

Na ___ na na na ___ na na. She be-longs to me.

Superheroes

Words and Music by Danny O'Donoghue, Mark Sheehan and James Barry

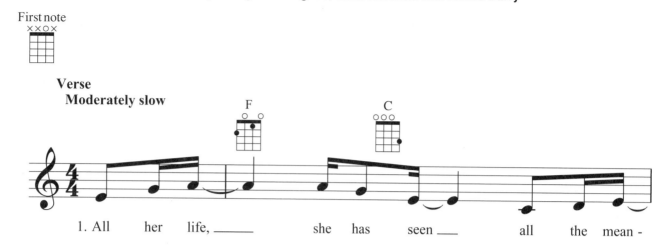

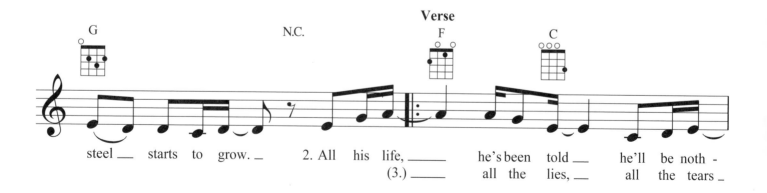

- ing when he's old. All the kicks and all the blows, he won't ev -
that they cry; when the mo - ment is just right, you see fi -

- er let it show. 'Cause he's strong -
- re in their eyes.

- er than you know; a heart of

steel starts to grow. When you've been fight - ing for it

𝄋 Chorus

all your life, you've been strug - gl - ing to

59

make things _ right, _ that's how a su - per - he - ro learns to _ fly. _____ (Ev - 'ry

day, ev - 'ry ho - ur, turn their pain in - to pow - er.) When you've been fight - ing for it

all your _ life, _____ you've been work - ing ev - 'ry

day and _ night, _ that's how a su - per - he - ro learns to _ fly. _____ (Ev - 'ry

1.

day, ev - 'ry ho - ur, turn their pain in - to pow - er.)

(Oh, uh oh. _ Oh, oh, _ uh oh.) _ 3. All the hurt, _

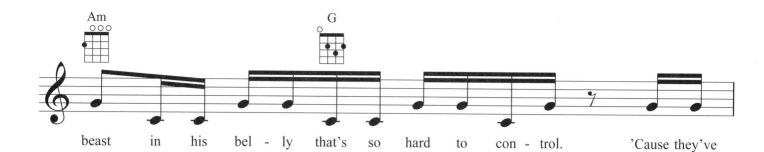

beast in his bel - ly that's so hard to con - trol. 'Cause they've

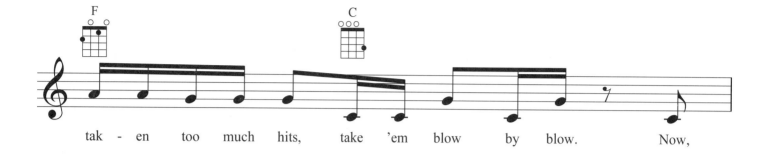

tak - en too much hits, take 'em blow by blow. Now,

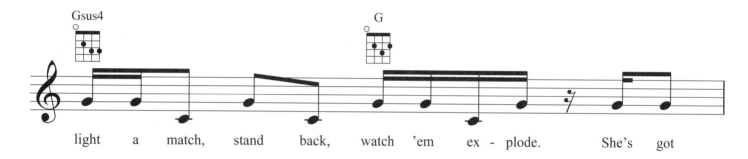

light a match, stand back, watch 'em ex - plode. She's got

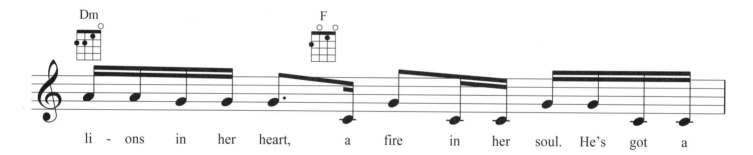

li - ons in her heart, a fire in her soul. He's got a

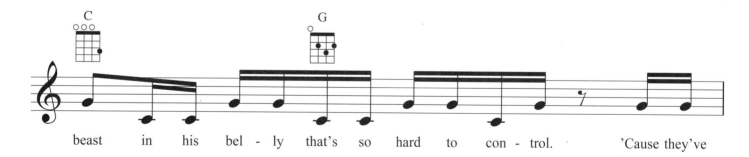

beast in his bel - ly that's so hard to con - trol. 'Cause they've

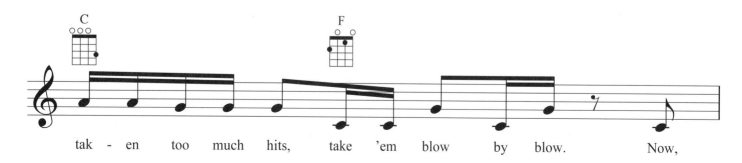

tak - en too much hits, take 'em blow by blow. Now,

light a match, stand back, watch 'em ex - plode, ___ ex - plode,

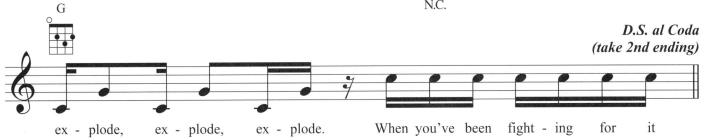

ex - plode, ex - plode, ex - plode. When you've been fight - ing for it

day, ev - 'ry ho - ur, turn their pain in - to pow - er.)
When you've been fight - ing for it

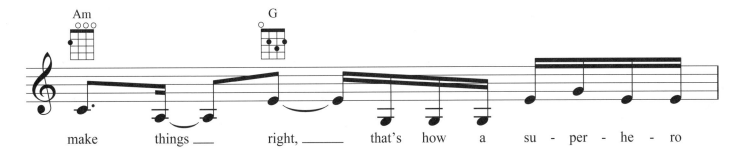

all your ___ life, ___ you've been strug - gl - ing to

make things ___ right, ___ that's how a su - per - he - ro

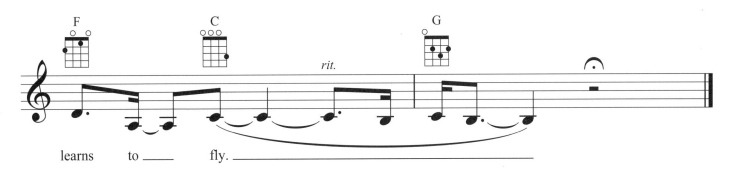

learns to ___ fly. ___

Take Me to Church

Words and Music by Andrew Hozier-Byrne

First note

Verse
Moderate Ballad

1. My lov-er's got hu-mor. She's the gig-gle at a fu-n'ral.

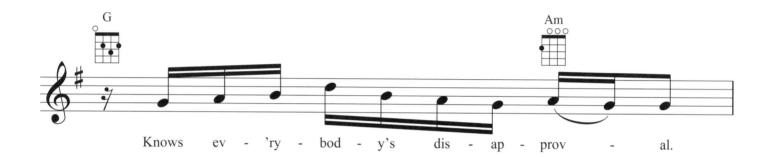

Knows ev-'ry-bod-y's dis-ap-prov-al.

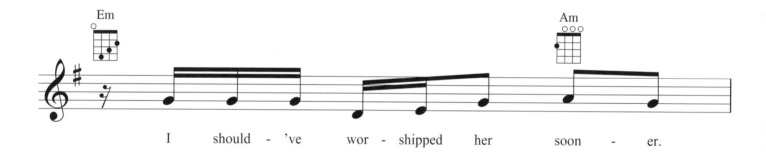

I should-'ve wor-shipped her soon-er.

If the heav-ens ev-er did speak, she's the last __ true mouth-piece.

Ev - 'ry Sun - day's get - ting more bleak, a fresh poi - son each week.

We were born ___ sick; you heard them ___ say it.

My church of - fers no ___ ab - so - lutes. She tells me, "Wor - ship in the bed - room."

The on - ly heav - en I'll be sent to is when I'm a - lone with you.

I was born sick, but I love _ it. Com - mand me to be well. A -

Pre-Chorus

- a - men, a -

men, __ a - men. Take me to church, __

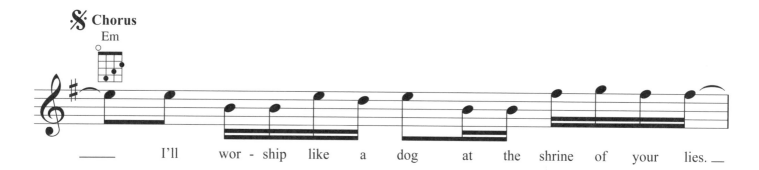

𝄌 Chorus

__ I'll wor - ship like a dog at the shrine of your lies. __

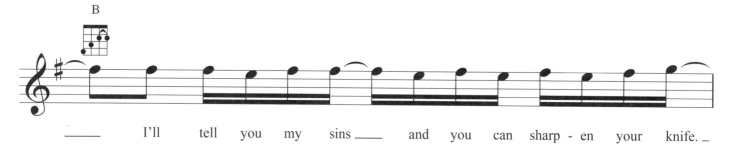

__ I'll tell you my sins __ and you can sharp - en your knife. __

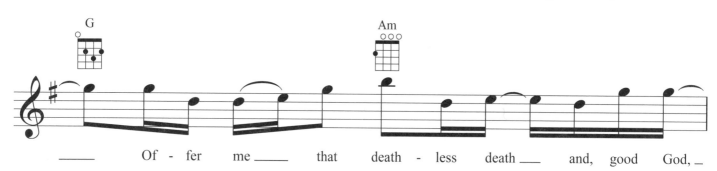

__ Of - fer me __ that death - less death __ and, good God, __

__ let me give you my life. Take me to church, __

__ I'll wor - ship like a dog at the shrine of your lies, __

I'll tell you my sins ___ and you can sharp - en your knife. ___

Of - fer me ___ that death - less death ___ and, good God, ___

To Coda 1 Verse
To Coda 2

___ let me give you my life.   2. If I'm a pa - gan of the good times,

my ___ lov - er's the sun - light.   To keep the god - dess on my ___ side,

she de - mands a sac - ri - fice.   Drain the whole sea,   get some - thing shin - y.

Some - thing meat - y for the main course,   that's a fine - look - ing high horse.

What you got in the sta - ble? — We've a lot of starv-ing faith - ful.

D.S. al Coda 1

That looks tast - y, that looks plen - ty. This is hun-gry work. _ Take me to church, _

Coda 1

_____ let me give you my life.

Bridge

No mas - ters _ or kings _ when the rit - u - al _____ be-gins. There is

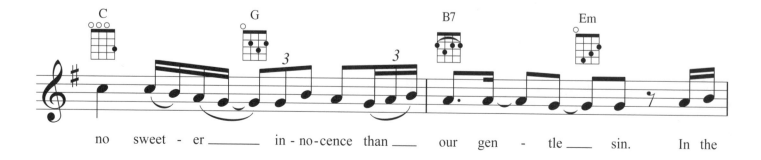

no sweet - er _____ in - no-cence than ___ our gen - tle ___ sin. In the

mad - ness ___ and soil   of that ___ sad ___ earth - ly scene,   on - ly

then I ___ am ___ hu - man,   on - ly   then   I ___ am ___

Pre-Chorus

___ clean. _   Oh, ___   oh, ___ a -

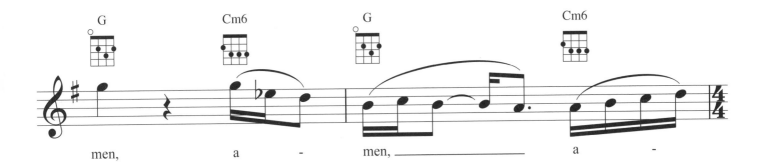

men,   a -   men, ___   a -

D.S. al Coda 2

men. ___   Take me to church, _

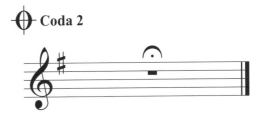

Coda 2

A Sky Full of Stars

Words and Music by Guy Berryman, Jon Buckland, Will Champion, Chris Martin and Tim Bergling

you. _____

Outro

'Cause you're a sky, _____ you're a sky _____ full of stars, _

_____ such a heav - en - ly view. _____

_____ You're such a heav - en - ly view. _____

_____ *(Instrumental)*

Play 3 times